Why bad Things Happen?

The Book that explains it all

A M Pellizzeri

Dedication

To those who look for answers and those
who just don't give a fuck.

Forward

Have you ever wondered to yourself or openly sought the answers to questions that begin with why?

The answer may seem obvious to some, totally wrong to others yet as you read it, and apply it to every negative event you've ever encountered personally or just read or heard about, you'll find that in your community, your nation, your world, and universe covering past, present and **ALL** future events as they unfold, the wisdom of its truth will astound and amaze you.

Preface

The human condition is one of **complex simplicity, convoluted logic, object poverty, immense wealth, harsh reality, surrealism, incomprehensible depravity, deliberate cruelty and random violence** we've all wondered why bad things happen. Disease and natural disasters can strike anyone, at anytime regardless of religious belief, social status or party affiliation, but do they? **YES** there is no divine or mystic rhyme or reason to it eventually we're all touched by tragedy and misfortune. We all succumb to the passage of time; **period**; death is an inevitable part of life. We must accept these things as the price we pay for having the privilege of cognitive awareness.. Random instances of chaos are often attributed to bad luck, god's will, natural selection, illegal immigration, or climate change but real reason for such events, has been left unexplained. **Until now!** The questions of evil, meanness, bad judgment and idiocy have an answer and through many years of study and observation, **I have found it!** More importantly I'm ready to share that answer with you.

Introduction

So here it is the answer to it all, from the beginning of time to today every bad thing, (as defined by your own personal morality), forever explained, every human act, of war, of terror, assaults, robbery, rape, murder, j walking, etc. A mass killing here, a rude waiter there, big and small noteworthy and mundane all acts of human behavior finally and forever explained. Take this knowledge with you and share it with those you know and those who have filled your head with complex lies and distortions. They will think you blasphemous and un-trainable. Be prepared to be sent to a re-education camp, or to your room without supper. To some this answer may seem trivial or obvious, an affirmation of belief a call to arms, a mantra, or battle cries? The all of human existence distilled into its true essence. Welcome to the new age of harsh reality and acceptance. Wonder no more. All is to be revealed. Your life is about to change. Enjoy.

The world is a fucked up place, filled with fucked up people, who do fucked up things for fucked up reasons.

Keep reading till it sinks in.

The world is a fucked up place, filled with fucked up people, who do fucked up things for fucked up reasons. The world is a fucked up place, filled with fucked up people, who do fucked up things for fucked up reasons. The world is a fucked up place, filled with fucked up people, who do fucked up things for fucked up reasons The world is a fucked up place, filled with fucked up people, who do fucked up things for fucked up reasons. The world is a fucked up place, filled with fucked up people, who do fucked up things for fucked up reasons. The world is a fucked up place, filled with fucked up people, who do fucked up things for fucked up reasons. The world is a fucked up place, filled with fucked up people, who do fucked up things for fucked up reasons. The world is a fucked up place, filled with fucked up people, who do fucked up things for fucked up reasons. The world is a fucked up place, filled with fucked up people, who do fucked up things for fucked up reasons. The world is a fucked up place, filled with fucked up people, who do fucked up things for fucked up reasons. The world is a fucked up place, filled with

fucked up people, who do fucked up things for fucked up reasons The world is a fucked up place, filled with fucked up people, who do fucked up things for fucked up reasons. The world is a fucked up place, filled with fucked up people, who do fucked up things for fucked up reasons. The world is a fucked up place, filled with fucked up people, who do fucked up things for fucked up reasons. The world is a fucked up place, filled with fucked up people, who do fucked up things for fucked up reasons The world is a fucked up place, filled with fucked up people, who do fucked up things for fucked up reasons. The world is a fucked up place, filled with fucked up people, who do fucked up things for fucked up reasons. The world is a fucked up place, filled with fucked up people, who do fucked up things for fucked up reasons. The world is a fucked up place, filled with fucked up people, who do fucked up things for fucked up reasons The world is a fucked up place, filled with fucked up people, who do fucked up things for fucked up reasons. The world is a fucked up place, filled with fucked up people, who do fucked up things for fucked up reasons. The world is a fucked up place, filled with fucked up people, who do fucked up things for fucked up reasons. The world is a fucked up place, filled with fucked up people, who do fucked up things for fucked up reasons. The world is a fucked

up place, filled with fucked up people, who do fucked up things for fucked up reasons. The world is a fucked up place, filled with fucked up people, who do fucked up things for fucked up reasons. The world is a fucked up place, filled with fucked up people, who do fucked up things for fucked up reasons. The world is a fucked up place, filled with fucked up people, who do fucked up things for fucked up reasons The world is a fucked up place, filled with fucked up people, who do fucked up things for fucked up reasons. The world is a fucked up place, filled with fucked up people, who do fucked up things for fucked up reasons. The world is a fucked up place, filled with fucked up people, who do fucked up things for fucked up reasons. The world is a fucked up place, filled with fucked up people, who do fucked up things for fucked up reasons. The world is a fucked up place, filled with fucked up people, who do fucked up things for fucked up reasons. The world is a fucked up place, filled with fucked up people, who do fucked up things for fucked up reasons. The world is a fucked up place, filled with fucked up people, who do fucked up things for fucked up reasons. The world is a fucked up place, filled with fucked up people, who do fucked up things for fucked up reasons The world is a fucked up place, filled with fucked up people, who do fucked up things for fucked up reasons.

The world is a fucked up place, filled with fucked up people, who do fucked up things for fucked up reasons. The world is a fucked up place, filled with fucked up people, who do fucked up things for fucked up reasons. The world is a fucked up place, filled with fucked up people, who do fucked up things for fucked up reasons. The world is a fucked up place, filled with fucked up people, who do fucked up things for fucked up reasons. The world is a fucked up place, filled with fucked up people, who do fucked up things for fucked up reasons. The world is a fucked up place, filled with fucked up people, who do fucked up things for fucked up reasons. The world is a fucked up place, filled with fucked up people, who do fucked up things for fucked up reasons The world is a fucked up place, filled with fucked up people, who do fucked up things for fucked up reasons. The world is a fucked up place, filled with fucked up people, who do fucked up things for fucked up reasons. The world is a fucked up place, filled with fucked up people, who do fucked up things for fucked up reasons. The world is a fucked up place, filled with fucked up people, who do fucked up things for fucked up reasons The world is a fucked up place, filled with fucked up people, who do fucked up things for fucked up reasons. The world is a fucked up place, filled with fucked up people, who do fucked up things

for fucked up reasons. The world is a fucked up place, filled with fucked up people, who do fucked up things for fucked up reasons. The world is a fucked up place, filled with fucked up people, who do fucked up things for fucked up reasons The world is a fucked up place, filled with fucked up people, who do fucked up things for fucked up reasons. The world is a fucked up place, filled with fucked up people, who do fucked up things for fucked up reasons. The world is a fucked up place, filled with fucked up people, who do fucked up things for fucked up reasons. The world is a fucked up place, filled with fucked up people, who do fucked up things for fucked up reasons. The world is a fucked up place, filled with fucked up people, who do fucked up things for fucked up reasons. The world is a fucked up place, filled with fucked up people, who do fucked up things for fucked up reasons. The world is a fucked up place, filled with fucked up people, who do fucked up things for fucked up reasons. The world is a fucked up place, filled with fucked up people, who do fucked up things for fucked up reasons The world is a fucked up place, filled with fucked up people, who do fucked up things for fucked up reasons. The world is a fucked up place, filled with fucked up people, who do fucked up things for fucked up reasons. The world is a fucked up place, filled with fucked up people, who

do fucked up things for fucked up reasons. The world is a fucked up place, filled with fucked up people, who do fucked up things for fucked up reasons. The world is a fucked up place, filled with fucked up people, who do fucked up things for fucked up reasons. The world is a fucked up place, filled with fucked up people, who do fucked up things for fucked up reasons. The world is a fucked up place, filled with fucked up people, who do fucked up things for fucked up reasons. The world is a fucked up place, filled with fucked up people, who do fucked up things for fucked up reasons The world is a fucked up place, filled with fucked up people, who do fucked up things for fucked up reasons. The world is a fucked up place, filled with fucked up people, who do fucked up things for fucked up reasons. The world is a fucked up place, filled with fucked up people, who do fucked up things for fucked up reasons. The world is a fucked up place, filled with fucked up people, who do fucked up things for fucked up reasons. The world is a fucked up place, filled with fucked up people, who do fucked up things for fucked up reasons. The world is a fucked up place, filled with fucked up people, who do fucked up things for fucked up reasons. The world is a fucked up place, filled with fucked up people, who do fucked up things for fucked up reasons. The world is a fucked up place, filled with

fucked up people, who do fucked up things for fucked up reasons The world is a fucked up place, filled with fucked up people, who do fucked up things for fucked up reasons. The world is a fucked up place, filled with fucked up people, who do fucked up things for fucked up reasons. The world is a fucked up place, filled with fucked up people, who do fucked up things for fucked up reasons. The world is a fucked up place, filled with fucked up people, who do fucked up things for fucked up reasons The world is a fucked up place, filled with fucked up people, who do fucked up things for fucked up reasons. The world is a fucked up place, filled with fucked up people, who do fucked up things for fucked up reasons. The world is a fucked up place, filled with fucked up people, who do fucked up things for fucked up reasons. The world is a fucked up place, filled with fucked up people, who do fucked up things for fucked up reasons The world is a fucked up place, filled with fucked up people, who do fucked up things for fucked up reasons. The world is a fucked up place, filled with fucked up people, who do fucked up things for fucked up reasons. The world is a fucked up place, filled with fucked up people, who do fucked up things for fucked up reasons. The world is a fucked up place, filled with fucked up people, who do fucked up things for fucked up reasons. The world is a fucked

up place, filled with fucked up people, who do fucked up things for fucked up reasons. The world is a fucked up place, filled with fucked up people, who do fucked up things for fucked up reasons. The world is a fucked up place, filled with fucked up people, who do fucked up things for fucked up reasons. The world is a fucked up place, filled with fucked up people, who do fucked up things for fucked up reasons The world is a fucked up place, filled with fucked up people, who do fucked up things for fucked up reasons. The world is a fucked up place, filled with fucked up people, who do fucked up things for fucked up reasons. The world is a fucked up place, filled with fucked up people, who do fucked up things for fucked up reasons. The world is a fucked up place, filled with fucked up people, who do fucked up things for fucked up reasons. The world is a fucked up place, filled with fucked up people, who do fucked up things for fucked up reasons. The world is a fucked up place, filled with fucked up people, who do fucked up things for fucked up reasons. The world is a fucked up place, filled with fucked up people, who do fucked up things for fucked up reasons. The world is a fucked up place, filled with fucked up people, who do fucked up things for fucked up reasons The world is a fucked up place, filled with fucked up people, who do fucked up things for fucked up reasons.

The world is a fucked up place, filled with fucked up people, who do fucked up things for fucked up reasons. The world is a fucked up place, filled with fucked up people, who do fucked up things for fucked up reasons. The world is a fucked up place, filled with fucked up people, who do fucked up things for fucked up reasons. The world is a fucked up place, filled with fucked up people, who do fucked up things for fucked up reasons. The world is a fucked up place, filled with fucked up people, who do fucked up things for fucked up reasons. The world is a fucked up place, filled with fucked up people, who do fucked up things for fucked up reasons. The world is a fucked up place, filled with fucked up people, who do fucked up things for fucked up reasons The world is a fucked up place, filled with fucked up people, who do fucked up things for fucked up reasons. The world is a fucked up place, filled with fucked up people, who do fucked up things for fucked up reasons. The world is a fucked up place, filled with fucked up people, who do fucked up things for fucked up reasons. The world is a fucked up place, filled with fucked up people, who do fucked up things for fucked up reasons The world is a fucked up place, filled with fucked up people, who do fucked up things for fucked up reasons. The world is a fucked up place, filled with fucked up people, who do fucked up things

for fucked up reasons. The world is a fucked up place, filled with fucked up people, who do fucked up things for fucked up reasons. The world is a fucked up place, filled with fucked up people, who do fucked up things for fucked up reasons The world is a fucked up place, filled with fucked up people, who do fucked up things for fucked up reasons. The world is a fucked up place, filled with fucked up people, who do fucked up things for fucked up reasons. The world is a fucked up place, filled with fucked up people, who do fucked up things for fucked up reasons. The world is a fucked up place, filled with fucked up people, who do fucked up things for fucked up reasons. The world is a fucked up place, filled with fucked up people, who do fucked up things for fucked up reasons. The world is a fucked up place, filled with fucked up people, who do fucked up things for fucked up reasons. The world is a fucked up place, filled with fucked up people, who do fucked up things for fucked up reasons. The world is a fucked up place, filled with fucked up people, who do fucked up things for fucked up reasons The world is a fucked up place, filled with fucked up people, who do fucked up things for fucked up reasons. The world is a fucked up place, filled with fucked up people, who do fucked up things for fucked up reasons. The world is a fucked up place, filled with fucked up people, who

do fucked up things for fucked up reasons. The world is a fucked up place, filled with fucked up people, who do fucked up things for fucked up reasons. The world is a fucked up place, filled with fucked up people, who do fucked up things for fucked up reasons. The world is a fucked up place, filled with fucked up people, who do fucked up things for fucked up reasons. The world is a fucked up place, filled with fucked up people, who do fucked up things for fucked up reasons. The world is a fucked up place, filled with fucked up people, who do fucked up things for fucked up reasons The world is a fucked up place, filled with fucked up people, who do fucked up things for fucked up reasons. The world is a fucked up place, filled with fucked up people, who do fucked up things for fucked up reasons. The world is a fucked up place, filled with fucked up people, who do fucked up things for fucked up reasons. The world is a fucked up place, filled with fucked up people, who do fucked up things for fucked up reasons. The world is a fucked up place, filled with fucked up people, who do fucked up things for fucked up reasons. The world is a fucked up place, filled with fucked up people, who do fucked up things for fucked up reasons. The world is a fucked up place, filled with fucked up people, who do fucked up things for fucked up reasons. The world is a fucked up place, filled with

fucked up people, who do fucked up things
for fucked up reasons The world is a fucked
up place, filled with fucked up people, who
do fucked up things for fucked up reasons.
The world is a fucked up place, filled with
fucked up people, who do fucked up things
for fucked up reasons. The world is a fucked
up place, filled with fucked up people, who
do fucked up things for fucked up reasons.
The world is a fucked up place, filled with
fucked up people, who do fucked up things
for fucked up reasons The world is a fucked
up place, filled with fucked up people, who
do fucked up things for fucked up reasons.
The world is a fucked up place, filled with
fucked up people, who do fucked up things
for fucked up reasons. The world is a fucked
up place, filled with fucked up people, who
do fucked up things for fucked up reasons.
The world is a fucked up place, filled with
fucked up people, who do fucked up things
for fucked up reasons The world is a fucked
up place, filled with fucked up people, who
do fucked up things for fucked up reasons.
The world is a fucked up place, filled with
fucked up people, who do fucked up things
for fucked up reasons. The world is a fucked
up place, filled with fucked up people, who
do fucked up things for fucked up reasons.
The world is a fucked up place, filled with
fucked up people, who do fucked up things
for fucked up reasons. The world is a fucked

up place, filled with fucked up people, who do fucked up things for fucked up reasons. The world is a fucked up place, filled with fucked up people, who do fucked up things for fucked up reasons. The world is a fucked up place, filled with fucked up people, who do fucked up things for fucked up reasons. The world is a fucked up place, filled with fucked up people, who do fucked up things for fucked up reasons The world is a fucked up place, filled with fucked up people, who do fucked up things for fucked up reasons. The world is a fucked up place, filled with fucked up people, who do fucked up things for fucked up reasons. The world is a fucked up place, filled with fucked up people, who do fucked up things for fucked up reasons. The world is a fucked up place, filled with fucked up people, who do fucked up things for fucked up reasons. The world is a fucked up place, filled with fucked up people, who do fucked up things for fucked up reasons. The world is a fucked up place, filled with fucked up people, who do fucked up things for fucked up reasons. The world is a fucked up place, filled with fucked up people, who do fucked up things for fucked up reasons. The world is a fucked up place, filled with fucked up people, who do fucked up things for fucked up reasons The world is a fucked up place, filled with fucked up people, who do fucked up things for fucked up reasons.

The world is a fucked up place, filled with fucked up people, who do fucked up things for fucked up reasons. The world is a fucked up place, filled with fucked up people, who do fucked up things for fucked up reasons. The world is a fucked up place, filled with fucked up people, who do fucked up things for fucked up reasons. The world is a fucked up place, filled with fucked up people, who do fucked up things for fucked up reasons. The world is a fucked up place, filled with fucked up people, who do fucked up things for fucked up reasons. The world is a fucked up place, filled with fucked up people, who do fucked up things for fucked up reasons. The world is a fucked up place, filled with fucked up people, who do fucked up things for fucked up reasons The world is a fucked up place, filled with fucked up people, who do fucked up things for fucked up reasons. The world is a fucked up place, filled with fucked up people, who do fucked up things for fucked up reasons. The world is a fucked up place, filled with fucked up people, who do fucked up things for fucked up reasons. The world is a fucked up place, filled with fucked up people, who do fucked up things for fucked up reasons The world is a fucked up place, filled with fucked up people, who do fucked up things for fucked up reasons. The world is a fucked up place, filled with fucked up people, who do fucked up things

for fucked up reasons. The world is a fucked up place, filled with fucked up people, who do fucked up things for fucked up reasons. The world is a fucked up place, filled with fucked up people, who do fucked up things for fucked up reasons The world is a fucked up place, filled with fucked up people, who do fucked up things for fucked up reasons. The world is a fucked up place, filled with fucked up people, who do fucked up things for fucked up reasons. The world is a fucked up place, filled with fucked up people, who do fucked up things for fucked up reasons. The world is a fucked up place, filled with fucked up people, who do fucked up things for fucked up reasons. The world is a fucked up place, filled with fucked up people, who do fucked up things for fucked up reasons. The world is a fucked up place, filled with fucked up people, who do fucked up things for fucked up reasons. The world is a fucked up place, filled with fucked up people, who do fucked up things for fucked up reasons. The world is a fucked up place, filled with fucked up people, who do fucked up things for fucked up reasons The world is a fucked up place, filled with fucked up people, who do fucked up things for fucked up reasons. The world is a fucked up place, filled with fucked up people, who do fucked up things for fucked up reasons. The world is a fucked up place, filled with fucked up people, who

do fucked up things for fucked up reasons. The world is a fucked up place, filled with fucked up people, who do fucked up things for fucked up reasons. The world is a fucked up place, filled with fucked up people, who do fucked up things for fucked up reasons. The world is a fucked up place, filled with fucked up people, who do fucked up things for fucked up reasons. The world is a fucked up place, filled with fucked up people, who do fucked up things for fucked up reasons. The world is a fucked up place, filled with fucked up people, who do fucked up things for fucked up reasons The world is a fucked up place, filled with fucked up people, who do fucked up things for fucked up reasons. The world is a fucked up place, filled with fucked up people, who do fucked up things for fucked up reasons. The world is a fucked up place, filled with fucked up people, who do fucked up things for fucked up reasons. The world is a fucked up place, filled with fucked up people, who do fucked up things for fucked up reasons. The world is a fucked up place, filled with fucked up people, who do fucked up things for fucked up reasons. The world is a fucked up place, filled with fucked up people, who do fucked up things for fucked up reasons. The world is a fucked up place, filled with fucked up people, who do fucked up things for fucked up reasons. The world is a fucked up place, filled with

fucked up people, who do fucked up things for fucked up reasons The world is a fucked up place, filled with fucked up people, who do fucked up things for fucked up reasons. The world is a fucked up place, filled with fucked up people, who do fucked up things for fucked up reasons. The world is a fucked up place, filled with fucked up people, who do fucked up things for fucked up reasons. The world is a fucked up place, filled with fucked up people, who do fucked up things for fucked up reasons The world is a fucked up place, filled with fucked up people, who do fucked up things for fucked up reasons. The world is a fucked up place, filled with fucked up people, who do fucked up things for fucked up reasons. The world is a fucked up place, filled with fucked up people, who do fucked up things for fucked up reasons. The world is a fucked up place, filled with fucked up people, who do fucked up things for fucked up reasons The world is a fucked up place, filled with fucked up people, who do fucked up things for fucked up reasons. The world is a fucked up place, filled with fucked up people, who do fucked up things for fucked up reasons. The world is a fucked up place, filled with fucked up people, who do fucked up things for fucked up reasons. The world is a fucked up place, filled with fucked up people, who do fucked up things for fucked up reasons. The world is a fucked

up place, filled with fucked up people, who do fucked up things for fucked up reasons. The world is a fucked up place, filled with fucked up people, who do fucked up things for fucked up reasons. The world is a fucked up place, filled with fucked up people, who do fucked up things for fucked up reasons. The world is a fucked up place, filled with fucked up people, who do fucked up things for fucked up reasons The world is a fucked up place, filled with fucked up people, who do fucked up things for fucked up reasons. The world is a fucked up place, filled with fucked up people, who do fucked up things for fucked up reasons. The world is a fucked up place, filled with fucked up people, who do fucked up things for fucked up reasons. The world is a fucked up place, filled with fucked up people, who do fucked up things for fucked up reasons. The world is a fucked up place, filled with fucked up people, who do fucked up things for fucked up reasons. The world is a fucked up place, filled with fucked up people, who do fucked up things for fucked up reasons. The world is a fucked up place, filled with fucked up people, who do fucked up things for fucked up reasons The world is a fucked up place, filled with fucked up people, who do fucked up things for fucked up reasons.

The world is a fucked up place, filled with fucked up people, who do fucked up things for fucked up reasons. The world is a fucked up place, filled with fucked up people, who do fucked up things for fucked up reasons. The world is a fucked up place, filled with fucked up people, who do fucked up things for fucked up reasons. The world is a fucked up place, filled with fucked up people, who do fucked up things for fucked up reasons. The world is a fucked up place, filled with fucked up people, who do fucked up things for fucked up reasons. The world is a fucked up place, filled with fucked up people, who do fucked up things for fucked up reasons. The world is a fucked up place, filled with fucked up people, who do fucked up things for fucked up reasons The world is a fucked up place, filled with fucked up people, who do fucked up things for fucked up reasons. The world is a fucked up place, filled with fucked up people, who do fucked up things for fucked up reasons. The world is a fucked up place, filled with fucked up people, who do fucked up things for fucked up reasons. The world is a fucked up place, filled with fucked up people, who do fucked up things for fucked up reasons The world is a fucked up place, filled with fucked up people, who do fucked up things for fucked up reasons. The world is a fucked up place, filled with fucked up people, who do fucked up things

for fucked up reasons. The world is a fucked up place, filled with fucked up people, who do fucked up things for fucked up reasons. The world is a fucked up place, filled with fucked up people, who do fucked up things for fucked up reasons The world is a fucked up place, filled with fucked up people, who do fucked up things for fucked up reasons. The world is a fucked up place, filled with fucked up people, who do fucked up things for fucked up reasons. The world is a fucked up place, filled with fucked up people, who do fucked up things for fucked up reasons. The world is a fucked up place, filled with fucked up people, who do fucked up things for fucked up reasons. The world is a fucked up place, filled with fucked up people, who do fucked up things for fucked up reasons. The world is a fucked up place, filled with fucked up people, who do fucked up things for fucked up reasons. The world is a fucked up place, filled with fucked up people, who do fucked up things for fucked up reasons The world is a fucked up place, filled with fucked up people, who do fucked up things for fucked up reasons. The world is a fucked up place, filled with fucked up people, who do fucked up things for fucked up reasons. The world is a fucked up place, filled with fucked up people, who

do fucked up things for fucked up reasons. The world is a fucked up place, filled with fucked up people, who do fucked up things for fucked up reasons. The world is a fucked up place, filled with fucked up people, who do fucked up things for fucked up reasons. The world is a fucked up place, filled with fucked up people, who do fucked up things for fucked up reasons. The world is a fucked up place, filled with fucked up people, who do fucked up things for fucked up reasons. The world is a fucked up place, filled with fucked up people, who do fucked up things for fucked up reasons The world is a fucked up place, filled with fucked up people, who do fucked up things for fucked up reasons. The world is a fucked up place, filled with fucked up people, who do fucked up things for fucked up reasons. The world is a fucked up place, filled with fucked up people, who do fucked up things for fucked up reasons. The world is a fucked up place, filled with fucked up people, who do fucked up things for fucked up reasons. The world is a fucked up place, filled with fucked up people, who do fucked up things for fucked up reasons. The world is a fucked up place, filled with fucked up people, who do fucked up things for fucked up reasons. The world is a fucked up place, filled with fucked up people, who do fucked up things for fucked up reasons. The world is a fucked up place, filled with

fucked up people, who do fucked up things for fucked up reasons The world is a fucked up place, filled with fucked up people, who do fucked up things for fucked up reasons. The world is a fucked up place, filled with fucked up people, who do fucked up things for fucked up reasons. The world is a fucked up place, filled with fucked up people, who do fucked up things for fucked up reasons. The world is a fucked up place, filled with fucked up people, who do fucked up things for fucked up reasons The world is a fucked up place, filled with fucked up people, who do fucked up things for fucked up reasons. The world is a fucked up place, filled with fucked up people, who do fucked up things for fucked up reasons. The world is a fucked up place, filled with fucked up people, who do fucked up things for fucked up reasons. The world is a fucked up place, filled with fucked up people, who do fucked up things for fucked up reasons The world is a fucked up place, filled with fucked up people, who do fucked up things for fucked up reasons. The world is a fucked up place, filled with fucked up people, who do fucked up things for fucked up reasons. The world is a fucked up place, filled with fucked up people, who do fucked up things for fucked up reasons.

It should be dawning on you about now that maybe **the world is a fucked up place, filled with fucked up people, that do**

fucked up things, for fucked up reasons. Also just maybe seeking clarity of thought and applying logic to the thoughts and actions of others is a waste of your time and effort.

If you have as of yet NOT reached that conclusion keep reading...

The world is a fucked up place, filled with fucked up people, who do fucked up things for fucked up reasons. The world is a fucked up place, filled with fucked up people, who do fucked up things for fucked up reasons. The world is a fucked up place, filled with fucked up people, who do fucked up things for fucked up reasons. The world is a fucked up place, filled with fucked up people, who do fucked up things for fucked up reasons. The world is a fucked up place, filled with fucked up people, who do fucked up things for fucked up reasons The world is a fucked up place, filled with fucked up people, who do fucked up things for fucked up reasons. The world is a fucked up place, filled with fucked up people, who do fucked up things for fucked up reasons. The world is a fucked up place, filled with fucked up people, who do fucked up things for fucked up reasons. The world is a fucked up place, filled with fucked up people, who do fucked up things for fucked up reasons. The world is a fucked

up place, filled with fucked up people, who do fucked up things for fucked up reasons. The world is a fucked up place, filled with fucked up people, who do fucked up things for fucked up reasons. The world is a fucked up place, filled with fucked up people, who do fucked up things for fucked up reasons. The world is a fucked up place, filled with fucked up people, who do fucked up things for fucked up reasons The world is a fucked up place, filled with fucked up people, who do fucked up things for fucked up reasons. The world is a fucked up place, filled with fucked up people, who do fucked up things for fucked up reasons. The world is a fucked up place, filled with fucked up people, who do fucked up things for fucked up reasons. The world is a fucked up place, filled with fucked up people, who do fucked up things for fucked up reasons. The world is a fucked up place, filled with fucked up people, who do fucked up things for fucked up reasons. The world is a fucked up place, filled with fucked up people, who do fucked up things for fucked up reasons. The world is a fucked up place, filled with fucked up people, who do fucked up things for fucked up reasons. The world is a fucked up place, filled with fucked up people, who do fucked up things for fucked up reasons The world is a fucked up place, filled with fucked up people, who do fucked up things for fucked up reasons.

The world is a fucked up place, filled with fucked up people, who do fucked up things for fucked up reasons. The world is a fucked up place, filled with fucked up people, who do fucked up things for fucked up reasons. The world is a fucked up place, filled with fucked up people, who do fucked up things for fucked up reasons The world is a fucked up place, filled with fucked up people, who do fucked up things for fucked up reasons. The world is a fucked up place, filled with fucked up people, who do fucked up things for fucked up reasons. The world is a fucked up place, filled with fucked up people, who do fucked up things for fucked up reasons. The world is a fucked up place, filled with fucked up people, who do fucked up things for fucked up reasons The world is a fucked up place, filled with fucked up people, who do fucked up things for fucked up reasons. The world is a fucked up place, filled with fucked up people, who do fucked up things for fucked up reasons. The world is a fucked up place, filled with fucked up people, who do fucked up things for fucked up reasons. The world is a fucked up place, filled with fucked up people, who do fucked up things for fucked up reasons. The world is a fucked up place, filled with fucked up people, who do fucked up things for fucked up reasons. The world is a fucked up place, filled with fucked up people, who do fucked up things for fucked up reasons. The world is a fucked up place, filled with fucked up people, who do fucked up things

for fucked up reasons. The world is a fucked up place, filled with fucked up people, who do fucked up things for fucked up reasons. The world is a fucked up place, filled with fucked up people, who do fucked up things for fucked up reasons The world is a fucked up place, filled with fucked up people, who do fucked up things for fucked up reasons. The world is a fucked up place, filled with fucked up people, who do fucked up things for fucked up reasons. The world is a fucked up place, filled with fucked up people, who do fucked up things for fucked up reasons. The world is a fucked up place, filled with fucked up people, who do fucked up things for fucked up reasons. The world is a fucked up place, filled with fucked up people, who do fucked up things for fucked up reasons. The world is a fucked up place, filled with fucked up people, who do fucked up things for fucked up reasons. The world is a fucked up place, filled with fucked up people, who do fucked up things for fucked up reasons. The world is a fucked up place, filled with fucked up people, who do fucked up things for fucked up reasons The world is a fucked up place, filled with fucked up people, who do fucked up things for fucked up reasons. The world is a fucked up place, filled with fucked up people, who do fucked up things for fucked up reasons. The world is a fucked up place, filled with fucked up people, who

do fucked up things for fucked up reasons.
The world is a fucked up place, filled with
fucked up people, who do fucked up things
for fucked up reasons. The world is a fucked
up place, filled with fucked up people, who
do fucked up things for fucked up reasons.
The world is a fucked up place, filled with
fucked up people, who do fucked up things
for fucked up reasons. The world is a fucked
up place, filled with fucked up people, who
do fucked up things for fucked up reasons.
The world is a fucked up place, filled with
fucked up people, who do fucked up things
for fucked up reasons The world is a fucked
up place, filled with fucked up people, who
do fucked up things for fucked up reasons.
The world is a fucked up place, filled with
fucked up people, who do fucked up things
for fucked up reasons. The world is a fucked
up place, filled with fucked up people, who
do fucked up things for fucked up reasons.
The world is a fucked up place, filled with
fucked up people, who do fucked up things
for fucked up reasons The world is a fucked
up place, filled with fucked up people, who
do fucked up things for fucked up reasons.
The world is a fucked up place, filled with
fucked up people, who do fucked up things
for fucked up reasons. The world is a fucked
up place, filled with fucked up people, who
do fucked up things for fucked up reasons.
The world is a fucked up place, filled with

fucked up people, who do fucked up things for fucked up reasons The world is a fucked up place, filled with fucked up people, who do fucked up things for fucked up reasons. The world is a fucked up place, filled with fucked up people, who do fucked up things for fucked up reasons. The world is a fucked up place, filled with fucked up people, who do fucked up things for fucked up reasons. The world is a fucked up place, filled with fucked up people, who do fucked up things for fucked up reasons. The world is a fucked up place, filled with fucked up people, who do fucked up things for fucked up reasons. The world is a fucked up place, filled with fucked up people, who do fucked up things for fucked up reasons. The world is a fucked up place, filled with fucked up people, who do fucked up things for fucked up reasons. The world is a fucked up place, filled with fucked up people, who do fucked up things for fucked up reasons The world is a fucked up place, filled with fucked up people, who do fucked up things for fucked up reasons. The world is a fucked up place, filled with fucked up people, who do fucked up things for fucked up reasons. The world is a fucked up place, filled with fucked up people, who do fucked up things for fucked up reasons.
 By now even the most optimistic amoung you must realize **the world is a fucked up place, filled with fucked up people, that**

**do fucked up things, for fucked up
reasons.**

If still in denial or holding out hope for an
enlightened Utopian awakening in the
hearts and minds of your fellow beings keep
reading...

The world is a fucked up place, filled with
fucked up people, who do fucked up things
for fucked up reasons The world is a fucked
up place, filled with fucked up people, who
do fucked up things for fucked up reasons.
The world is a fucked up place, filled with
fucked up people, who do fucked up things
for fucked up reasons. The world is a fucked
up place, filled with fucked up people, who
do fucked up things for fucked up reasons.
The world is a fucked up place, filled with
fucked up people, who do fucked up things
for fucked up reasons The world is a fucked
up place, filled with fucked up people, who
do fucked up things for fucked up reasons.
The world is a fucked up place, filled with
fucked up people, who do fucked up things
for fucked up reasons. The world is a fucked
up place, filled with fucked up people, who
do fucked up things for fucked up reasons.
The world is a fucked up place, filled with
fucked up people, who do fucked up things
for fucked up reasons. The world is a fucked
up place, filled with fucked up people, who

do fucked up things for fucked up reasons. The world is a fucked up place, filled with fucked up people, who do fucked up things for fucked up reasons. The world is a fucked up place, filled with fucked up people, who do fucked up things for fucked up reasons. The world is a fucked up place, filled with fucked up people, who do fucked up things for fucked up reasons The world is a fucked up place, filled with fucked up people, who do fucked up things for fucked up reasons. The world is a fucked up place, filled with fucked up people, who do fucked up things for fucked up reasons. The world is a fucked up place, filled with fucked up people, who do fucked up things for fucked up reasons. The world is a fucked up place, filled with fucked up people, who do fucked up things for fucked up reasons The world is a fucked up place, filled with fucked up people, who do fucked up things for fucked up reasons. The world is a fucked up place, filled with fucked up people, who do fucked up things for fucked up reasons. The world is a fucked up place, filled with fucked up people, who do fucked up things for fucked up reasons. The world is a fucked up place, filled with fucked up people, who do fucked up things for fucked up reasons The world is a fucked up place, filled with fucked up people, who do fucked up things for fucked up reasons. The world is a fucked up place, filled with

fucked up people, who do fucked up things
for fucked up reasons. The world is a fucked
up place, filled with fucked up people, who
do fucked up things for fucked up reasons.
The world is a fucked up place, filled with
fucked up people, who do fucked up things
for fucked up reasons. The world is a fucked
up place, filled with fucked up people, who
do fucked up things for fucked up reasons.
The world is a fucked up place, filled with
fucked up people, who do fucked up things
for fucked up reasons. The world is a fucked
up place, filled with fucked up people, who
do fucked up things for fucked up reasons.
The world is a fucked up place, filled with
fucked up people, who do fucked up things
for fucked up reasons The world is a fucked
up place, filled with fucked up people, who
do fucked up things for fucked up reasons.
The world is a fucked up place, filled with
fucked up people, who do fucked up things
for fucked up reasons. The world is a fucked
up place, filled with fucked up people, who
do fucked up things for fucked up reasons.
The world is a fucked up place, filled with
fucked up people, who do fucked up things
for fucked up reasons. The world is a fucked
up place, filled with fucked up people, who
do fucked up things for fucked up reasons.
The world is a fucked up place, filled with
fucked up people, who do fucked up things
for fucked up reasons. The world is a fucked

up place, filled with fucked up people, who do fucked up things for fucked up reasons. The world is a fucked up place, filled with fucked up people, who do fucked up things for fucked up reasons The world is a fucked up place, filled with fucked up people, who do fucked up things for fucked up reasons. The world is a fucked up place, filled with fucked up people, who do fucked up things for fucked up reasons. The world is a fucked up place, filled with fucked up people, who do fucked up things for fucked up reasons. The world is a fucked up place, filled with fucked up people, who do fucked up things for fucked up reasons. The world is a fucked up place, filled with fucked up people, who do fucked up things for fucked up reasons. The world is a fucked up place, filled with fucked up people, who do fucked up things for fucked up reasons. The world is a fucked up place, filled with fucked up people, who do fucked up things for fucked up reasons. The world is a fucked up place, filled with fucked up people, who do fucked up things for fucked up reasons. The world is a fucked up place, filled with fucked up people, who do fucked up things for fucked up reasons The world is a fucked up place, filled with fucked up people, who do fucked up things for fucked up reasons. The world is a fucked up place, filled with fucked up people, who do fucked up things for fucked up reasons. The world is a fucked up place, filled with fucked up people, who do fucked up things for fucked up reasons.

The world is a fucked up place, filled with
fucked up people, who do fucked up things
for fucked up reasons The world is a fucked
up place, filled with fucked up people, who
do fucked up things for fucked up reasons.
The world is a fucked up place, filled with
fucked up people, who do fucked up things
for fucked up reasons. The world is a fucked
up place, filled with fucked up people, who
do fucked up things for fucked up reasons.
The world is a fucked up place, filled with
fucked up people, who do fucked up things
for fucked up reasons The world is a fucked
up place, filled with fucked up people, who
do fucked up things for fucked up reasons.
The world is a fucked up place, filled with
fucked up people, who do fucked up things
for fucked up reasons. The world is a fucked
up place, filled with fucked up people, who
do fucked up things for fucked up reasons.
The world is a fucked up place, filled with
fucked up people, who do fucked up things
for fucked up reasons. The world is a fucked
up place, filled with fucked up people, who
do fucked up things for fucked up reasons.
The world is a fucked up place, filled with
fucked up people, who do fucked up things
for fucked up reasons. The world is a fucked
up place, filled with fucked up people, who
do fucked up things for fucked up reasons.
The world is a fucked up place, filled with
fucked up people, who do fucked up things

for fucked up reasons The world is a fucked up place, filled with fucked up people, who do fucked up things for fucked up reasons. The world is a fucked up place, filled with fucked up people, who do fucked up things for fucked up reasons. The world is a fucked up place, filled with fucked up people, who do fucked up things for fucked up reasons. The world is a fucked up place, filled with fucked up people, who do fucked up things for fucked up reasons The world is a fucked up place, filled with fucked up people, who do fucked up things for fucked up reasons. The world is a fucked up place, filled with fucked up people, who do fucked up things for fucked up reasons. The world is a fucked up place, filled with fucked up people, who do fucked up things for fucked up reasons. The world is a fucked up place, filled with fucked up people, who do fucked up things for fucked up reasons The world is a fucked up place, filled with fucked up people, who do fucked up things for fucked up reasons. The world is a fucked up place, filled with fucked up people, who do fucked up things for fucked up reasons. The world is a fucked up place, filled with fucked up people, who do fucked up things for fucked up reasons. The world is a fucked up place, filled with fucked up people, who do fucked up things for fucked up reasons. The world is a fucked up place, filled with fucked up people, who

do fucked up things for fucked up reasons. The world is a fucked up place, filled with fucked up people, who do fucked up things for fucked up reasons. The world is a fucked up place, filled with fucked up people, who do fucked up things for fucked up reasons. The world is a fucked up place, filled with fucked up people, who do fucked up things for fucked up reasons The world is a fucked up place, filled with fucked up people, who do fucked up things for fucked up reasons. The world is a fucked up place, filled with fucked up people, who do fucked up things for fucked up reasons. The world is a fucked up place, filled with fucked up people, who do fucked up things for fucked up reasons. The world is a fucked up place, filled with fucked up people, who do fucked up things for fucked up reasons The world is a fucked up place, filled with fucked up people, who do fucked up things for fucked up reasons. The world is a fucked up place, filled with fucked up people, who do fucked up things for fucked up reasons. The world is a fucked up place, filled with fucked up people, who do fucked up things for fucked up reasons. The world is a fucked up place, filled with fucked up people, who do fucked up things for fucked up reasons The world is a fucked up place, filled with fucked up people, who do fucked up things for fucked up reasons. The world is a fucked up place, filled with

fucked up people, who do fucked up things for fucked up reasons. The world is a fucked up place, filled with fucked up people, who do fucked up things for fucked up reasons. The world is a fucked up place, filled with fucked up people, who do fucked up things for fucked up reasons. The world is a fucked up place, filled with fucked up people, who do fucked up things for fucked up reasons. The world is a fucked up place, filled with fucked up people, who do fucked up things for fucked up reasons. The world is a fucked up place, filled with fucked up people, who do fucked up things for fucked up reasons. The world is a fucked up place, filled with fucked up people, who do fucked up things for fucked up reasons The world is a fucked up place, filled with fucked up people, who do fucked up things for fucked up reasons. The world is a fucked up place, filled with fucked up people, who do fucked up things for fucked up reasons. The world is a fucked up place, filled with fucked up people, who do fucked up things for fucked up reasons. The world is a fucked up place, filled with fucked up people, who do fucked up things for fucked up reasons. The world is a fucked up place, filled with fucked up people, who do fucked up things for fucked up reasons.
Sometimes you have to accept the reality of negative situations, doesn't mean you give up, or give in, just acknowledge the

motivation of the elephant in the room, and move on.

If this still hasn't sunk in keep reading…

The world is a fucked up place, filled with fucked up people, who do fucked up things for fucked up reasons. The world is a fucked up place, filled with fucked up people, who do fucked up things for fucked up reasons. The world is a fucked up place, filled with fucked up people, who do fucked up things for fucked up reasons The world is a fucked up place, filled with fucked up people, who do fucked up things for fucked up reasons. The world is a fucked up place, filled with fucked up people, who do fucked up things for fucked up reasons. The world is a fucked up place, filled with fucked up people, who do fucked up things for fucked up reasons. The world is a fucked up place, filled with fucked up people, who do fucked up things for fucked up reasons. The world is a fucked up place, filled with fucked up people, who do fucked up things for fucked up reasons. The world is a fucked up place, filled with fucked up people, who do fucked up things for fucked up reasons. The world is a fucked up place, filled with fucked up people, who do fucked up things for fucked up reasons. The world is a fucked up place, filled with fucked up people, who do fucked up things for fucked up reasons The world is a fucked up place, filled with fucked up people, who do fucked up things for fucked up reasons. The world is a fucked up place, filled with fucked up people, who do fucked up things for fucked up reasons. The world is a fucked up place, filled with fucked up people, who do fucked up things for fucked up reasons. The world is a fucked up place, filled with fucked up people, who do fucked up things for fucked up reasons The world is a fucked up place, filled with fucked up people, who do fucked up things for fucked up reasons. The world is a fucked up place, filled with fucked up people, who do fucked up things for fucked up reasons. The world is a fucked up place, filled with fucked up people, who do fucked up things for fucked up reasons. The world is a fucked up place, filled with fucked up people, who do fucked up things for fucked up reasons The world is a fucked up place, filled with fucked up people, who do fucked up things for fucked up reasons. The world is a fucked up place, filled with fucked up people, who do fucked up things for fucked up reasons. The world is a fucked up place, filled with fucked up people, who do fucked up things for fucked up reasons. The world is a fucked up place, filled with fucked up people, who do fucked up things for fucked up reasons. The world is a fucked up place, filled with fucked up people, who

do fucked up things for fucked up reasons. The world is a fucked up place, filled with fucked up people, who do fucked up things for fucked up reasons. The world is a fucked up place, filled with fucked up people, who do fucked up things for fucked up reasons. The world is a fucked up place, filled with fucked up people, who do fucked up things for fucked up reasons The world is a fucked up place, filled with fucked up people, who do fucked up things for fucked up reasons. The world is a fucked up place, filled with fucked up people, who do fucked up things for fucked up reasons. The world is a fucked up place, filled with fucked up people, who do fucked up things for fucked up reasons. The world is a fucked up place, filled with fucked up people, who do fucked up things for fucked up reasons The world is a fucked up place, filled with fucked up people, who do fucked up things for fucked up reasons. The world is a fucked up place, filled with fucked up people, who do fucked up things for fucked up reasons. The world is a fucked up place, filled with fucked up people, who do fucked up things for fucked up reasons. The world is a fucked up place, filled with fucked up people, who do fucked up things for fucked up reasons The world is a fucked up place, filled with fucked up people, who do fucked up things for fucked up reasons. The world is a fucked up place, filled with

fucked up people, who do fucked up things for fucked up reasons. The world is a fucked up place, filled with fucked up people, who do fucked up things for fucked up reasons. The world is a fucked up place, filled with fucked up people, who do fucked up things for fucked up reasons. The world is a fucked up place, filled with fucked up people, who do fucked up things for fucked up reasons. The world is a fucked up place, filled with fucked up people, who do fucked up things for fucked up reasons. The world is a fucked up place, filled with fucked up people, who do fucked up things for fucked up reasons. The world is a fucked up place, filled with fucked up people, who do fucked up things for fucked up reasons The world is a fucked up place, filled with fucked up people, who do fucked up things for fucked up reasons. The world is a fucked up place, filled with fucked up people, who do fucked up things for fucked up reasons. The world is a fucked up place, filled with fucked up people, who do fucked up things for fucked up reasons. The world is a fucked up place, filled with fucked up people, who do fucked up things for fucked up reasons The world is a fucked up place, filled with fucked up people, who do fucked up things for fucked up reasons. The world is a fucked up place, filled with fucked up people, who do fucked up things for fucked up reasons. The world is a fucked up place, filled with fucked up people, who do fucked up things for fucked up reasons. The world is a fucked up place, filled with fucked up people, who do fucked up things for fucked up reasons The world is a fucked up place, filled with fucked up people, who do fucked up things for fucked up reasons. The world is a fucked up place, filled with fucked up people, who do fucked up things for fucked up reasons. The world is a fucked up place, filled with fucked up people, who do fucked up things for fucked up reasons.

The essence of philosophical thought is that the ability to reason should somehow lead us to inner and outer peace when in fact it's mankind's ability to follow blindly the fucked up thoughts of others that allows the former and dooms the latter. The world is a fucked up place, filled with fucked up people, who do fucked up things for fucked up reasons. The world is a fucked up place, filled with fucked up people, who do fucked up things for fucked up reasons. The world is a fucked up place, filled with fucked up people, who do fucked up things for fucked up reasons. The world is a fucked up place, filled with fucked up people, who do fucked up things for fucked up reasons. The world is a fucked up place, filled with fucked up people, who do fucked up things for fucked up reasons The world is a fucked up place, filled with fucked up people, who do fucked up things for fucked up reasons. The world is a fucked up place, filled with fucked up people, who do fucked up things for fucked up reasons. The world is a fucked up place, filled with fucked up people, who do fucked up things for fucked up reasons. The world is a fucked up place, filled with fucked up people, who do fucked up things for fucked up reasons. The world is a fucked up place, filled with fucked up people, who do fucked up things for fucked up reasons. The world is a fucked up place, filled with fucked up people, who do fucked up things for fucked up reasons. The world is a fucked up place, filled with fucked up people, who do fucked up things for fucked up reasons. The world is a fucked up place, filled with fucked up people, who do fucked up things for fucked up reasons The world is a fucked up place, filled with fucked up people, who do fucked up things for fucked up reasons. The world is a fucked up place, filled with fucked up people, who do fucked up things for fucked up reasons. The world is a fucked up place, filled with fucked up people, who do fucked up things for fucked up reasons. The world is a fucked up place, filled with fucked up people, who do fucked up things for fucked up reasons. The world is a fucked up place, filled with fucked up people, who do fucked up things for fucked up reasons. The world is a fucked up place, filled with fucked up people, who do fucked up things for fucked up reasons. The world is a fucked up place, filled with fucked up people, who do fucked up things for fucked up reasons. The world is a fucked up place, filled with fucked up people, who do fucked up things for fucked up reasons The world is a fucked up place, filled with fucked up people, who do fucked up things for fucked up reasons. The world is a fucked up place, filled with fucked up people, who do fucked up things for fucked up reasons. The world is a fucked up place, filled with fucked up people, who do fucked up things for fucked up reasons. The world is a fucked up place, filled with fucked up people, who do fucked up things for fucked up reasons The world is a fucked up place, filled with fucked up people, who do fucked up things for fucked up reasons. The world is a fucked up place, filled with fucked up people, who do fucked up things for fucked up reasons. The world is a fucked up place, filled with fucked up people, who do fucked up things for fucked up reasons. The world is a fucked up place, filled with fucked up people, who do fucked up things for fucked up reasons The world is a fucked up place, filled with fucked up people, who do fucked up things for fucked up reasons. The world is a fucked up place, filled with fucked up people, who do fucked up things for fucked up reasons The world is a fucked up place, filled with fucked up people, who do fucked up things for fucked up reasons. The world is a fucked up place, filled with fucked up people, who do fucked up things for fucked up reasons. The world is a fucked up place, filled with fucked up people, who do fucked up things for fucked up reasons. The world is a fucked up place, filled with fucked up people, who do fucked up things for fucked up reasons. The world is a fucked up place, filled with fucked up people, who do fucked up things for fucked up reasons. The world is a fucked up place, filled with fucked up people, who do fucked up things for fucked up reasons. The world is a fucked up place, filled with fucked up people, who do fucked up things for fucked up reasons. The world is a fucked up place, filled with fucked up people, who do fucked up things for fucked up reasons The world is a fucked up place, filled with fucked up people, who do fucked up things for fucked up reasons. The world is a fucked up place, filled with fucked up people, who do fucked up things for fucked up reasons. The world is a fucked up place, filled with fucked up people, who do fucked up things for fucked up reasons The world is a fucked up place, filled with fucked up people, who do fucked up things for fucked up reasons. The world is a fucked up place, filled with fucked up people, who do fucked up things for fucked up reasons. The world is a fucked up place, filled with fucked up people, who do fucked up things for fucked up reasons. The world is a fucked up place, filled with fucked up people, who do fucked up things for fucked up reasons The world is a fucked up place, filled with fucked up people, who do fucked up things for fucked up reasons. The world is a fucked up place, filled with fucked up people, who do fucked up things for fucked up reasons. The world is a fucked up place, filled with fucked up people, who do fucked up things for fucked up reasons. The world is a fucked up place, filled with fucked up people, who do fucked up things for fucked up reasons. The world is a fucked up place, filled with fucked up people, who do fucked up things for fucked up reasons. The world is a fucked up place, filled with fucked up people, who do fucked up things for fucked up reasons. The world is a fucked up place, filled with fucked up people, who do fucked up things for fucked up reasons. The world is a fucked up place, filled with fucked up people, who do fucked up things for fucked up reasons The world is a fucked up place, filled with fucked up people, who do fucked up things for fucked up reasons. The world is a fucked up place, filled with fucked up people, who do fucked up things for fucked up reasons. The world is a fucked up place, filled with fucked up people, who do fucked up things for fucked up reasons. The world is a fucked up place, filled with fucked up people, who do fucked up things for fucked up reasons

The world is a fucked up place, filled with fucked up people, who do fucked up things for fucked up reasons. The world is a fucked up place, filled with fucked up people, who do fucked up things for fucked up reasons. The world is a fucked up place, filled with fucked up people, who do fucked up things for fucked up reasons. The world is a fucked up place, filled with fucked up people, who do fucked up things for fucked up reasons The world is a fucked up place, filled with fucked up people, who do fucked up things for fucked up reasons. The world is a fucked up place, filled with fucked up people, who do fucked up things for fucked up reasons. The world is a fucked up place, filled with fucked up people, who do fucked up things for fucked up reasons. The world is a fucked up place, filled with fucked up people, who do fucked up things for fucked up reasons. The world is a fucked up place, filled with fucked up people, who do fucked up things for fucked up reasons. The world is a fucked up place, filled with fucked up people, who do fucked up things for fucked up reasons. The world is a fucked up place, filled with fucked up people, who do fucked up things for fucked up reasons. The world is a fucked up place, filled with fucked up people, who do fucked up things for fucked up reasons The world is a fucked up place, filled with fucked up people, who do fucked up things for fucked up reasons. The world is a fucked up place, filled with fucked up people, who do fucked up things for fucked up reasons. The world is a fucked up place, filled with fucked up people, who do fucked up things for fucked up reasons. The world is a fucked up place, filled with fucked up people, who do fucked up things for fucked up reasons. The world is a fucked up place, filled with fucked up people, who do fucked up things for fucked up reasons. The world is a fucked up place, filled with fucked up people, who do fucked up things for fucked up reasons. The world is a fucked up place, filled with fucked up people, who do fucked up things for fucked up reasons. The world is a fucked up place, filled with fucked up people, who do fucked up things for fucked up reasons The world is a fucked up place, filled with fucked up people, who do fucked up things for fucked up reasons. The world is a fucked up place, filled with fucked up people, who do fucked up things for fucked up reasons. The world is a fucked up place, filled with fucked up people, who do fucked up things for fucked up reasons. The world is a fucked up place, filled with fucked up people, who do fucked up things for fucked up reasons. The world is a fucked up place, filled with fucked up people, who do fucked up things for fucked up reasons. The world is a fucked up place, filled with fucked up people, who

do fucked up things for fucked up reasons.
The world is a fucked up place, filled with
fucked up people, who do fucked up things
for fucked up reasons. The world is a fucked
up place, filled with fucked up people, who
do fucked up things for fucked up reasons
The world is a fucked up place, filled with
fucked up people, who do fucked up things
for fucked up reasons. The world is a fucked
up place, filled with fucked up people, who
do fucked up things for fucked up reasons.
The world is a fucked up place, filled with
fucked up people, who do fucked up things
for fucked up reasons. The world is a fucked
up place, filled with fucked up people, who
do fucked up things for fucked up reasons
The world is a fucked up place, filled with
fucked up people, who do fucked up things
for fucked up reasons. The world is a fucked
up place, filled with fucked up people, who
do fucked up things for fucked up reasons.
The world is a fucked up place, filled with
fucked up people, who do fucked up things
for fucked up reasons. The world is a fucked
up place, filled with fucked up people, who
do fucked up things for fucked up reasons
The world is a fucked up place, filled with
fucked up people, who do fucked up things
for fucked up reasons. The world is a fucked
up place, filled with fucked up people, who
do fucked up things for fucked up reasons.
The world is a fucked up place, filled with

fucked up people, who do fucked up things for fucked up reasons. The world is a fucked up place, filled with fucked up people, who do fucked up things for fucked up reasons. The world is a fucked up place, filled with fucked up people, who do fucked up things for fucked up reasons. The world is a fucked up place, filled with fucked up people, who do fucked up things for fucked up reasons. The world is a fucked up place, filled with fucked up people, who do fucked up things for fucked up reasons. The world is a fucked up place, filled with fucked up people, who do fucked up things for fucked up reasons The world is a fucked up place, filled with fucked up people, who do fucked up things for fucked up reasons. The world is a fucked up place, filled with fucked up people, who do fucked up things for fucked up reasons. The world is a fucked up place, filled with fucked up people, who do fucked up things for fucked up reasons. The world is a fucked up place, filled with fucked up people, who do fucked up things for fucked up reasons The world is a fucked up place, filled with fucked up people, who do fucked up things for fucked up reasons. The world is a fucked up place, filled with fucked up people, who do fucked up things for fucked up reasons.
Maybe by now you're stating to realize that the world isn't run by some divine plan and

everything doesn't happen for a reason. (other than fucked up ones.)

Read on non-believer...

The world is a fucked up place, filled with fucked up people, who do fucked up things for fucked up reasons. The world is a fucked up place, filled with fucked up people, who do fucked up things for fucked up reasons The world is a fucked up place, filled with fucked up people, who do fucked up things for fucked up reasons. The world is a fucked up place, filled with fucked up people, who do fucked up things for fucked up reasons. The world is a fucked up place, filled with fucked up people, who do fucked up things for fucked up reasons. The world is a fucked up place, filled with fucked up people, who do fucked up things for fucked up reasons. The world is a fucked up place, filled with fucked up people, who do fucked up things for fucked up reasons. The world is a fucked up place, filled with fucked up people, who do fucked up things for fucked up reasons. The world is a fucked up place, filled with fucked up people, who do fucked up things for fucked up reasons. The world is a fucked up place, filled with fucked up people, who do fucked up things for fucked up reasons The world is a fucked up place, filled with fucked up people, who do fucked up things

for fucked up reasons. The world is a fucked up place, filled with fucked up people, who do fucked up things for fucked up reasons. The world is a fucked up place, filled with fucked up people, who do fucked up things for fucked up reasons. The world is a fucked up place, filled with fucked up people, who do fucked up things for fucked up reasons
The world is a fucked up place, filled with fucked up people, who do fucked up things for fucked up reasons. The world is a fucked up place, filled with fucked up people, who do fucked up things for fucked up reasons. The world is a fucked up place, filled with fucked up people, who do fucked up things for fucked up reasons. The world is a fucked up place, filled with fucked up people, who do fucked up things for fucked up reasons
The world is a fucked up place, filled with fucked up people, who do fucked up things for fucked up reasons. The world is a fucked up place, filled with fucked up people, who do fucked up things for fucked up reasons. The world is a fucked up place, filled with fucked up people, who do fucked up things for fucked up reasons. The world is a fucked up place, filled with fucked up people, who do fucked up things for fucked up reasons. The world is a fucked up place, filled with fucked up people, who

do fucked up things for fucked up reasons. The world is a fucked up place, filled with fucked up people, who do fucked up things for fucked up reasons. The world is a fucked up place, filled with fucked up people, who do fucked up things for fucked up reasons The world is a fucked up place, filled with fucked up people, who do fucked up things for fucked up reasons. The world is a fucked up place, filled with fucked up people, who do fucked up things for fucked up reasons. The world is a fucked up place, filled with fucked up people, who do fucked up things for fucked up reasons. The world is a fucked up place, filled with fucked up people, who do fucked up things for fucked up reasons. The world is a fucked up place, filled with fucked up people, who do fucked up things for fucked up reasons. The world is a fucked up place, filled with fucked up people, who do fucked up things for fucked up reasons. The world is a fucked up place, filled with fucked up people, who do fucked up things for fucked up reasons. The world is a fucked up place, filled with fucked up people, who do fucked up things for fucked up reasons The world is a fucked up place, filled with fucked up people, who do fucked up things for fucked up reasons. The world is a fucked up place, filled with fucked up people, who do fucked up things for fucked up reasons. The world is a fucked up place, filled with

fucked up people, who do fucked up things
for fucked up reasons. The world is a fucked
up place, filled with fucked up people, who
do fucked up things for fucked up reasons.
The world is a fucked up place, filled with
fucked up people, who do fucked up things
for fucked up reasons. The world is a fucked
up place, filled with fucked up people, who
do fucked up things for fucked up reasons.
The world is a fucked up place, filled with
fucked up people, who do fucked up things
for fucked up reasons. The world is a fucked
up place, filled with fucked up people, who
do fucked up things for fucked up reasons
The world is a fucked up place, filled with
fucked up people, who do fucked up things
for fucked up reasons. The world is a fucked
up place, filled with fucked up people, who
do fucked up things for fucked up reasons.
The world is a fucked up place, filled with
fucked up people, who do fucked up things
for fucked up reasons. The world is a fucked
up place, filled with fucked up people, who
do fucked up things for fucked up reasons
The world is a fucked up place, filled with
fucked up people, who do fucked up things
for fucked up reasons. The world is a fucked
up place, filled with fucked up people, who
do fucked up things for fucked up reasons.
The world is a fucked up place, filled with
fucked up people, who do fucked up things
for fucked up reasons. The world is a fucked

up place, filled with fucked up people, who do fucked up things for fucked up reasons The world is a fucked up place, filled with fucked up people, who do fucked up things for fucked up reasons. The world is a fucked up place, filled with fucked up people, who do fucked up things for fucked up reasons. The world is a fucked up place, filled with fucked up people, who do fucked up things for fucked up reasons. The world is a fucked up place, filled with fucked up people, who do fucked up things for fucked up reasons. The world is a fucked up place, filled with fucked up people, who do fucked up things for fucked up reasons. The world is a fucked up place, filled with fucked up people, who do fucked up things for fucked up reasons. The world is a fucked up place, filled with fucked up people, who do fucked up things for fucked up reasons. The world is a fucked up place, filled with fucked up people, who do fucked up things for fucked up reasons The world is a fucked up place, filled with fucked up people, who do fucked up things for fucked up reasons. The world is a fucked up place, filled with fucked up people, who do fucked up things for fucked up reasons. The world is a fucked up place, filled with fucked up people, who do fucked up things for fucked up reasons. The world is a fucked up place, filled with fucked up people, who do fucked up things for fucked up reasons

The world is a fucked up place, filled with
fucked up people, who do fucked up things
for fucked up reasons. The world is a fucked
up place, filled with fucked up people, who
do fucked up things for fucked up reasons.
The world is a fucked up place, filled with
fucked up people, who do fucked up things
for fucked up reasons. The world is a fucked
up place, filled with fucked up people, who
do fucked up things for fucked up reasons
The world is a fucked up place, filled with
fucked up people, who do fucked up things
for fucked up reasons. The world is a fucked
up place, filled with fucked up people, who
do fucked up things for fucked up reasons.
The world is a fucked up place, filled with
fucked up people, who do fucked up things
for fucked up reasons. The world is a fucked
up place, filled with fucked up people, who
do fucked up things for fucked up reasons.
The world is a fucked up place, filled with
fucked up people, who do fucked up things
for fucked up reasons. The world is a fucked
up place, filled with fucked up people, who
do fucked up things for fucked up reasons.
The world is a fucked up place, filled with
fucked up people, who do fucked up things
for fucked up reasons. The world is a fucked
up place, filled with fucked up people, who
do fucked up things for fucked up reasons
The world is a fucked up place, filled with
fucked up people, who do fucked up things

for fucked up reasons. The world is a fucked up place, filled with fucked up people, who do fucked up things for fucked up reasons. The world is a fucked up place, filled with fucked up people, who do fucked up things for fucked up reasons. The world is a fucked up place, filled with fucked up people, who do fucked up things for fucked up reasons
The world is a fucked up place, filled with fucked up people, who do fucked up things for fucked up reasons. The world is a fucked up place, filled with fucked up people, who do fucked up things for fucked up reasons. The world is a fucked up place, filled with fucked up people, who do fucked up things for fucked up reasons. The world is a fucked up place, filled with fucked up people, who do fucked up things for fucked up reasons
The world is a fucked up place, filled with fucked up people, who do fucked up things for fucked up reasons. The world is a fucked up place, filled with fucked up people, who do fucked up things for fucked up reasons. The world is a fucked up place, filled with fucked up people, who do fucked up things for fucked up reasons. The world is a fucked up place, filled with fucked up people, who do fucked up things for fucked up reasons. The world is a fucked up place, filled with fucked up people, who do fucked up things for fucked up reasons. The world is a fucked up place, filled with fucked up people, who

do fucked up things for fucked up reasons. The world is a fucked up place, filled with fucked up people, who do fucked up things for fucked up reasons. The world is a fucked up place, filled with fucked up people, who do fucked up things for fucked up reasons The world is a fucked up place, filled with fucked up people, who do fucked up things for fucked up reasons. The world is a fucked up place, filled with fucked up people, who do fucked up things for fucked up reasons. The world is a fucked up place, filled with fucked up people, who do fucked up things for fucked up reasons. The world is a fucked up place, filled with fucked up people, who do fucked up things for fucked up reasons. The world is a fucked up place, filled with fucked up people, who do fucked up things for fucked up reasons. The world is a fucked up place, filled with fucked up people, who do fucked up things for fucked up reasons. The world is a fucked up place, filled with fucked up people, who do fucked up things for fucked up reasons. The world is a fucked up place, filled with fucked up people, who do fucked up things for fucked up reasons The world is a fucked up place, filled with fucked up people, who do fucked up things for fucked up reasons. The world is a fucked up place, filled with fucked up people, who do fucked up things for fucked up reasons.

The world is a fucked up place, filled with fucked up people, who do fucked up things for fucked up reasons. The world is a fucked up place, filled with fucked up people, who do fucked up things for fucked up reasons. The world is a fucked up place, filled with fucked up people, who do fucked up things for fucked up reasons. The world is a fucked up place, filled with fucked up people, who do fucked up things for fucked up reasons. The world is a fucked up place, filled with fucked up people, who do fucked up things for fucked up reasons. The world is a fucked up place, filled with fucked up people, who do fucked up things for fucked up reasons The world is a fucked up place, filled with fucked up people, who do fucked up things for fucked up reasons. The world is a fucked up place, filled with fucked up people, who do fucked up things for fucked up reasons. The world is a fucked up place, filled with fucked up people, who do fucked up things for fucked up reasons. The world is a fucked up place, filled with fucked up people, who do fucked up things for fucked up reasons The world is a fucked up place, filled with fucked up people, who do fucked up things for fucked up reasons. The world is a fucked up place, filled with fucked up people, who do fucked up things for fucked up reasons. The world is a fucked up place, filled with fucked up people, who do fucked up things for fucked up reasons. The world is a fucked up place, filled with fucked up people, who do fucked up things for fucked up reasons The world is a fucked up place, filled with fucked up people, who do fucked up things for fucked up reasons. The world is a fucked up place, filled with fucked up people, who do fucked up things for fucked up reasons. The world is a fucked up place, filled with fucked up people, who do fucked up things for fucked up reasons. The world is a fucked up place, filled with fucked up people, who do fucked up things for fucked up reasons. The world is a fucked up place, filled with fucked up people, who do fucked up things for fucked up reasons. The world is a fucked up place, filled with fucked up people, who do fucked up things for fucked up reasons. The world is a fucked up place, filled with fucked up people, who do fucked up things for fucked up reasons The world is a fucked up place, filled with fucked up people, who do fucked up things for fucked up reasons. The world is a fucked up place, filled with fucked up people, who do fucked up things for fucked up reasons. The world is a fucked up place, filled with fucked up people, who do fucked up things for fucked up reasons. The world is a fucked up place, filled with fucked up people, who

do fucked up things for fucked up reasons
The world is a fucked up place, filled with
fucked up people, who do fucked up things
for fucked up reasons. The world is a fucked
up place, filled with fucked up people, who
do fucked up things for fucked up reasons.
The world is a fucked up place, filled with
fucked up people, who do fucked up things
for fucked up reasons. The world is a fucked
up place, filled with fucked up people, who
do fucked up things for fucked up reasons
The world is a fucked up place, filled with
fucked up people, who do fucked up things
for fucked up reasons. The world is a fucked
up place, filled with fucked up people, who
do fucked up things for fucked up reasons.
The world is a fucked up place, filled with
fucked up people, who do fucked up things
for fucked up reasons. The world is a fucked
up place, filled with fucked up people, who
do fucked up things for fucked up reasons.
The world is a fucked up place, filled with
fucked up people, who do fucked up things
for fucked up reasons. The world is a fucked
up place, filled with fucked up people, who
do fucked up things for fucked up reasons.
The world is a fucked up place, filled with
fucked up people, who do fucked up things
for fucked up reasons. The world is a fucked
up place, filled with fucked up people, who
do fucked up things for fucked up reasons.
The world is a fucked up place, filled with
fucked up people, who do fucked up things
for fucked up reasons. The world is a fucked
up place, filled with fucked up people, who
do fucked up things for fucked up reasons
The world is a fucked up place, filled with

fucked up people, who do fucked up things
for fucked up reasons. The world is a fucked
up place, filled with fucked up people, who
do fucked up things for fucked up reasons.
The world is a fucked up place, filled with
fucked up people, who do fucked up things
for fucked up reasons. The world is a fucked
up place, filled with fucked up people, who
do fucked up things for fucked up reasons
The world is a fucked up place, filled with
fucked up people, who do fucked up things
for fucked up reasons. The world is a fucked
up place, filled with fucked up people, who
do fucked up things for fucked up reasons.
The world is a fucked up place, filled with
fucked up people, who do fucked up things
for fucked up reasons. The world is a fucked
up place, filled with fucked up people, who
do fucked up things for fucked up reasons
The world is a fucked up place, filled with
fucked up people, who do fucked up things
for fucked up reasons. The world is a fucked
up place, filled with fucked up people, who
do fucked up things for fucked up reasons.
The world is a fucked up place, filled with
fucked up people, who do fucked up things
for fucked up reasons. The world is a fucked
up place, filled with fucked up people, who
do fucked up things for fucked up reasons.
The world is a fucked up place, filled with
fucked up people, who do fucked up things
for fucked up reasons. The world is a fucked

up place, filled with fucked up people, who do fucked up things for fucked up reasons. The world is a fucked up place, filled with fucked up people, who do fucked up things for fucked up reasons. The world is a fucked up place, filled with fucked up people, who do fucked up things for fucked up reasons The world is a fucked up place, filled with fucked up people, who do fucked up things for fucked up reasons. The world is a fucked up place, filled with fucked up people, who do fucked up things for fucked up reasons. The world is a fucked up place, filled with fucked up people, who do fucked up things for fucked up reasons. The world is a fucked up place, filled with fucked up people, who do fucked up things for fucked up reasons. The world is a fucked up place, filled with fucked up people, who do fucked up things for fucked up reasons. The world is a fucked up place, filled with fucked up people, who do fucked up things for fucked up reasons. The world is a fucked up place, filled with fucked up people, who do fucked up things for fucked up reasons. The world is a fucked up place, filled with fucked up people, who do fucked up things for fucked up reasons. The world is a fucked up place, filled with fucked up people, who do fucked up things for fucked up reasons The world is a fucked up place, filled with fucked up people, who do fucked up things for fucked up reasons. The world is a fucked up place, filled with fucked up people, who do fucked up things for fucked up reasons.

The world is a fucked up place, filled with fucked up people, who do fucked up things for fucked up reasons. The world is a fucked up place, filled with fucked up people, who do fucked up things for fucked up reasons. The world is a fucked up place, filled with fucked up people, who do fucked up things for fucked up reasons. The world is a fucked up place, filled with fucked up people, who do fucked up things for fucked up reasons. The world is a fucked up place, filled with fucked up people, who do fucked up things for fucked up reasons. The world is a fucked up place, filled with fucked up people, who do fucked up things for fucked up reasons The world is a fucked up place, filled with fucked up people, who do fucked up things for fucked up reasons. The world is a fucked up place, filled with fucked up people, who do fucked up things for fucked up reasons. The world is a fucked up place, filled with fucked up people, who do fucked up things for fucked up reasons. The world is a fucked up place, filled with fucked up people, who do fucked up things for fucked up reasons The world is a fucked up place, filled with fucked up people, who do fucked up things for fucked up reasons. The world is a fucked up place, filled with fucked up people, who do fucked up things for fucked up reasons.

Cause and effect applied to chains of random events come together to form the genesis of progressive reality. We all see the same thing but our brains perceive it differently.

This perception makes the most sense...

The world is a fucked up place, filled with fucked up people, who do fucked up things for fucked up reasons. The world is a fucked up place, filled with fucked up people, who do fucked up things for fucked up reasons The world is a fucked up place, filled with fucked up people, who do fucked up things for fucked up reasons. The world is a fucked up place, filled with fucked up people, who do fucked up things for fucked up reasons. The world is a fucked up place, filled with fucked up people, who do fucked up things for fucked up reasons. The world is a fucked up place, filled with fucked up people, who do fucked up things for fucked up reasons. The world is a fucked up place, filled with fucked up people, who do fucked up things for fucked up reasons. The world is a fucked up place, filled with fucked up people, who do fucked up things for fucked up reasons. The world is a fucked up place, filled with fucked up people, who do fucked up things for fucked up reasons. The world is a fucked up place, filled with fucked up people, who

do fucked up things for fucked up reasons
The world is a fucked up place, filled with
fucked up people, who do fucked up things
for fucked up reasons. The world is a fucked
up place, filled with fucked up people, who
do fucked up things for fucked up reasons.
The world is a fucked up place, filled with
fucked up people, who do fucked up things
for fucked up reasons. The world is a fucked
up place, filled with fucked up people, who
do fucked up things for fucked up reasons
The world is a fucked up place, filled with
fucked up people, who do fucked up things
for fucked up reasons. The world is a fucked
up place, filled with fucked up people, who
do fucked up things for fucked up reasons.
The world is a fucked up place, filled with
fucked up people, who do fucked up things
for fucked up reasons. The world is a fucked
up place, filled with fucked up people, who
do fucked up things for fucked up reasons
The world is a fucked up place, filled with
fucked up people, who do fucked up things
for fucked up reasons. The world is a fucked
up place, filled with fucked up people, who
do fucked up things for fucked up reasons.
The world is a fucked up place, filled with
fucked up people, who do fucked up things
for fucked up reasons. The world is a fucked
up place, filled with fucked up people, who
do fucked up things for fucked up reasons.
The world is a fucked up place, filled with

fucked up people, who do fucked up things for fucked up reasons. The world is a fucked up place, filled with fucked up people, who do fucked up things for fucked up reasons. The world is a fucked up place, filled with fucked up people, who do fucked up things for fucked up reasons. The world is a fucked up place, filled with fucked up people, who do fucked up things for fucked up reasons The world is a fucked up place, filled with fucked up people, who do fucked up things for fucked up reasons. The world is a fucked up place, filled with fucked up people, who do fucked up things for fucked up reasons. The world is a fucked up place, filled with fucked up people, who do fucked up things for fucked up reasons. The world is a fucked up place, filled with fucked up people, who do fucked up things for fucked up reasons The world is a fucked up place, filled with fucked up people, who do fucked up things for fucked up reasons. The world is a fucked up place, filled with fucked up people, who do fucked up things for fucked up reasons. The world is a fucked up place, filled with fucked up people, who do fucked up things for fucked up reasons. The world is a fucked up place, filled with fucked up people, who do fucked up things for fucked up reasons The world is a fucked up place, filled with fucked up people, who do fucked up things for fucked up reasons. The world is a fucked

up place, filled with fucked up people, who do fucked up things for fucked up reasons.
The world is a fucked up place, filled with fucked up people, who do fucked up things for fucked up reasons. The world is a fucked up place, filled with fucked up people, who do fucked up things for fucked up reasons. The world is a fucked up place, filled with fucked up people, who do fucked up things for fucked up reasons. The world is a fucked up place, filled with fucked up people, who do fucked up things for fucked up reasons. The world is a fucked up place, filled with fucked up people, who do fucked up things for fucked up reasons. The world is a fucked up place, filled with fucked up people, who do fucked up things for fucked up reasons The world is a fucked up place, filled with fucked up people, who do fucked up things for fucked up reasons. The world is a fucked up place, filled with fucked up people, who do fucked up things for fucked up reasons. The world is a fucked up place, filled with fucked up people, who do fucked up things for fucked up reasons. The world is a fucked up place, filled with fucked up people, who do fucked up things for fucked up reasons. The world is a fucked up place, filled with fucked up people, who do fucked up things for fucked up reasons. The world is a fucked up place, filled with fucked up people, who do fucked up things for fucked up reasons.

The world is a fucked up place, filled with
fucked up people, who do fucked up things
for fucked up reasons. The world is a fucked
up place, filled with fucked up people, who
do fucked up things for fucked up reasons
The world is a fucked up place, filled with
fucked up people, who do fucked up things
for fucked up reasons. The world is a fucked
up place, filled with fucked up people, who
do fucked up things for fucked up reasons.
The world is a fucked up place, filled with
fucked up people, who do fucked up things
for fucked up reasons. The world is a fucked
up place, filled with fucked up people, who
do fucked up things for fucked up reasons.
The world is a fucked up place, filled with
fucked up people, who do fucked up things
for fucked up reasons. The world is a fucked
up place, filled with fucked up people, who
do fucked up things for fucked up reasons.
The world is a fucked up place, filled with
fucked up people, who do fucked up things
for fucked up reasons. The world is a fucked
up place, filled with fucked up people, who
do fucked up things for fucked up reasons
The world is a fucked up place, filled with
fucked up people, who do fucked up things
for fucked up reasons. The world is a fucked
up place, filled with fucked up people, who
do fucked up things for fucked up reasons.
The world is a fucked up place, filled with
fucked up people, who do fucked up things

for fucked up reasons. The world is a fucked up place, filled with fucked up people, who do fucked up things for fucked up reasons The world is a fucked up place, filled with fucked up people, who do fucked up things for fucked up reasons. The world is a fucked up place, filled with fucked up people, who do fucked up things for fucked up reasons. The world is a fucked up place, filled with fucked up people, who do fucked up things for fucked up reasons. The world is a fucked up place, filled with fucked up people, who do fucked up things for fucked up reasons The world is a fucked up place, filled with fucked up people, who do fucked up things for fucked up reasons. The world is a fucked up place, filled with fucked up people, who do fucked up things for fucked up reasons. The world is a fucked up place, filled with fucked up people, who do fucked up things for fucked up reasons. The world is a fucked up place, filled with fucked up people, who do fucked up things for fucked up reasons. The world is a fucked up place, filled with fucked up people, who do fucked up things for fucked up reasons. The world is a fucked up place, filled with fucked up people, who do fucked up things for fucked up reasons. The world is a fucked up place, filled with fucked up people, who do fucked up things for fucked up reasons. The world is a fucked up place, filled with fucked up people, who do fucked up things for fucked up reasons. The world is a fucked up place, filled with fucked up people, who

do fucked up things for fucked up reasons
The world is a fucked up place, filled with
fucked up people, who do fucked up things
for fucked up reasons. The world is a fucked
up place, filled with fucked up people, who
do fucked up things for fucked up reasons.
The world is a fucked up place, filled with
fucked up people, who do fucked up things
for fucked up reasons. The world is a fucked
up place, filled with fucked up people, who
do fucked up things for fucked up reasons
The world is a fucked up place, filled with
fucked up people, who do fucked up things
for fucked up reasons. The world is a fucked
up place, filled with fucked up people, who
do fucked up things for fucked up reasons.
The world is a fucked up place, filled with
fucked up people, who do fucked up things
for fucked up reasons. The world is a fucked
up place, filled with fucked up people, who
do fucked up things for fucked up reasons
The world is a fucked up place, filled with
fucked up people, who do fucked up things
for fucked up reasons. The world is a fucked
up place, filled with fucked up people, who
do fucked up things for fucked up reasons.
The world is a fucked up place, filled with
fucked up people, who do fucked up things
for fucked up reasons. The world is a fucked
up place, filled with fucked up people, who
do fucked up things for fucked up reasons.

If at this point you are still reading this I applaud your efforts yet question your work ethic and time management skills

Read on MacDuff...

The world is a fucked up place, filled with fucked up people, who do fucked up things for fucked up reasons. The world is a fucked up place, filled with fucked up people, who do fucked up things for fucked up reasons. The world is a fucked up place, filled with fucked up people, who do fucked up things for fucked up reasons. The world is a fucked up place, filled with fucked up people, who do fucked up things for fucked up reasons The world is a fucked up place, filled with fucked up people, who do fucked up things for fucked up reasons. The world is a fucked up place, filled with fucked up people, who do fucked up things for fucked up reasons. The world is a fucked up place, filled with fucked up people, who do fucked up things for fucked up reasons. The world is a fucked up place, filled with fucked up people, who do fucked up things for fucked up reasons The world is a fucked up place, filled with fucked up people, who do fucked up things for fucked up reasons. The world is a fucked up place, filled with fucked up people, who do fucked up things for fucked up reasons. The world is a fucked up place, filled with fucked up people, who do fucked up things for fucked up reasons. The world is a fucked up place, filled with fucked up people, who do fucked up things for fucked up reasons The world is a fucked up place, filled with fucked up people, who do fucked up things for fucked up reasons. The world is a fucked up place, filled with fucked up people, who do fucked up things for fucked up reasons. The world is a fucked up place, filled with fucked up people, who do fucked up things for fucked up reasons. The world is a fucked up place, filled with fucked up people, who do fucked up things for fucked up reasons. The world is a fucked up place, filled with fucked up people, who do fucked up things for fucked up reasons. The world is a fucked up place, filled with fucked up people, who do fucked up things for fucked up reasons. The world is a fucked up place, filled with fucked up people, who do fucked up things for fucked up reasons. The world is a fucked up place, filled with fucked up people, who do fucked up things for fucked up reasons The world is a fucked up place, filled with fucked up people, who do fucked up things for fucked up reasons. The world is a fucked up place, filled with fucked up people, who do fucked up things for fucked up reasons. The world is a fucked up place, filled with fucked up people, who do fucked up things for fucked up reasons. The world is a fucked

up place, filled with fucked up people, who do fucked up things for fucked up reasons.
The world is a fucked up place, filled with fucked up people, who do fucked up things for fucked up reasons. The world is a fucked up place, filled with fucked up people, who do fucked up things for fucked up reasons. The world is a fucked up place, filled with fucked up people, who do fucked up things for fucked up reasons. The world is a fucked up place, filled with fucked up people, who do fucked up things for fucked up reasons The world is a fucked up place, filled with fucked up people, who do fucked up things for fucked up reasons. The world is a fucked up place, filled with fucked up people, who do fucked up things for fucked up reasons. The world is a fucked up place, filled with fucked up people, who do fucked up things for fucked up reasons. The world is a fucked up place, filled with fucked up people, who do fucked up things for fucked up reasons. The world is a fucked up place, filled with fucked up people, who do fucked up things for fucked up reasons. The world is a fucked up place, filled with fucked up people, who do fucked up things for fucked up reasons. The world is a fucked up place, filled with fucked up people, who do fucked up things for fucked up reasons

The world is a fucked up place, filled with fucked up people, who do fucked up things for fucked up reasons. The world is a fucked up place, filled with fucked up people, who do fucked up things for fucked up reasons. The world is a fucked up place, filled with fucked up people, who do fucked up things for fucked up reasons. The world is a fucked up place, filled with fucked up people, who do fucked up things for fucked up reasons The world is a fucked up place, filled with fucked up people, who do fucked up things for fucked up reasons. The world is a fucked up place, filled with fucked up people, who do fucked up things for fucked up reasons. The world is a fucked up place, filled with fucked up people, who do fucked up things for fucked up reasons. The world is a fucked up place, filled with fucked up people, who do fucked up things for fucked up reasons The world is a fucked up place, filled with fucked up people, who do fucked up things for fucked up reasons. The world is a fucked up place, filled with fucked up people, who do fucked up things for fucked up reasons. The world is a fucked up place, filled with fucked up people, who do fucked up things for fucked up reasons. The world is a fucked up place, filled with fucked up people, who do fucked up things for fucked up reasons. The world is a fucked up place, filled with fucked up people, who do fucked up things for fucked up reasons. The world is a fucked up place, filled with fucked up people, who do fucked up things for fucked up reasons. The world is a fucked up place, filled with fucked up people, who do fucked up things for fucked up reasons. The world is a fucked up place, filled with fucked up people, who do fucked up things for fucked up reasons The world is a fucked up place, filled with fucked up people, who do fucked up things for fucked up reasons. The world is a fucked up place, filled with fucked up people, who do fucked up things for fucked up reasons. The world is a fucked up place, filled with fucked up people, who do fucked up things for fucked up reasons. The world is a fucked up place, filled with fucked up people, who do fucked up things for fucked up reasons The world is a fucked up place, filled with fucked up people, who do fucked up things for fucked up reasons. The world is a fucked up place, filled with fucked up people, who do fucked up things for fucked up reasons. The world is a fucked up place, filled with fucked up people, who do fucked up things for fucked up reasons. The world is a fucked up place, filled with fucked up people, who do fucked up things for fucked up reasons The world is a fucked up place, filled with fucked up people, who do fucked up things for fucked up reasons. The world is a fucked up place, filled with fucked up people, who do fucked up things for fucked up reasons. The world is a fucked up place, filled with fucked up people, who do fucked up things for fucked up reasons. The world is a fucked up place, filled with fucked up people, who do fucked up things for fucked up reasons. The world is a fucked up place, filled with fucked up people, who do fucked up things for fucked up reasons. The world is a fucked up place, filled with fucked up people, who do fucked up things for fucked up reasons. The world is a fucked up place, filled with fucked up people, who do fucked up things for fucked up reasons. The world is a fucked up place, filled with fucked up people, who do fucked up things for fucked up reasons The world is a fucked up place, filled with fucked up people, who do fucked up things for fucked up reasons. The world is a fucked up place, filled with fucked up people, who do fucked up things for fucked up reasons. The world is a fucked up place, filled with fucked up people, who do fucked up things for fucked up reasons The world is a fucked up place, filled with fucked up people, who do fucked up things for fucked up reasons. The world is a fucked up place, filled with fucked up people, who do fucked up things for fucked up reasons. The world is a fucked up place, filled with fucked up people, who do fucked up things for fucked up reasons. The world is a fucked up place, filled with fucked up people, who do fucked up things for fucked up reasons The world is a fucked up place, filled with fucked up people, who do fucked up things for fucked up reasons. The world is a fucked up place, filled with fucked up people, who do fucked up things for fucked up reasons. The world is a fucked up place, filled with fucked up people, who do fucked up things for fucked up reasons. The world is a fucked up place, filled with fucked up people, who do fucked up things for fucked up reasons. The world is a fucked up place, filled with fucked up people, who do fucked up things for fucked up reasons. The world is a fucked up place, filled with fucked up people, who do fucked up things for fucked up reasons. The world is a fucked up place, filled with fucked up people, who do fucked up things for fucked up reasons The world is a fucked up place, filled with fucked up people, who do fucked up things for fucked up reasons. The world is a fucked up place, filled with fucked up people, who do fucked up things for fucked up reasons. The world is a fucked up place, filled with fucked up people, who do fucked up things for fucked up reasons. The world is a fucked up place, filled with fucked up people, who do fucked up things for fucked up reasons. The world is a fucked up place, filled with fucked up people, who do fucked up things for fucked up reasons. The world is a fucked up place, filled with fucked up people, who do fucked up things for fucked up reasons. The world is a fucked up place, filled with fucked up people, who do fucked up things for fucked up reasons. The world is a fucked up place, filled with fucked up people, who do fucked up things for fucked up reasons The world is a fucked up place, filled with fucked up people, who do fucked up things for fucked up reasons. The world is a fucked up place, filled with fucked up people, who do fucked up things for fucked up reasons. The world is a fucked up place, filled with fucked up people, who do fucked up things for fucked up reasons. The world is a fucked up place, filled with fucked up people, who do fucked up things for fucked up reasons. The world is a fucked up place, filled with fucked up people, who do fucked up things for fucked up reasons. The world is a fucked up place, filled with fucked up people, who do fucked up things for fucked up reasons.

The acceptance of reality is the first step to understanding inner peace and intellectual freedom

My intellect plots against me; in my defense
I've killed off as many brain cells as possible
eventually I will level the playing field and it
will become an even fight

If you have yet to see the wisdom in
surrendering your object optimism, keep
reading…

The world is a fucked up place, filled with
fucked up people, who do fucked up things
for fucked up reasons. The world is a fucked
up place, filled with fucked up people, who
do fucked up things for fucked up reasons
The world is a fucked up place, filled with
fucked up people, who do fucked up things
for fucked up reasons. The world is a fucked
up place, filled with fucked up people, who
do fucked up things for fucked up reasons.
The world is a fucked up place, filled with
fucked up people, who do fucked up things
for fucked up reasons. The world is a fucked
up place, filled with fucked up people, who
do fucked up things for fucked up reasons
The world is a fucked up place, filled with
fucked up people, who do fucked up things
for fucked up reasons. The world is a fucked
up place, filled with fucked up people, who
do fucked up things for fucked up reasons.
The world is a fucked up place, filled with
fucked up people, who do fucked up things
for fucked up reasons. The world is a fucked

up place, filled with fucked up people, who do fucked up things for fucked up reasons The world is a fucked up place, filled with fucked up people, who do fucked up things for fucked up reasons. The world is a fucked up place, filled with fucked up people, who do fucked up things for fucked up reasons. The world is a fucked up place, filled with fucked up people, who do fucked up things for fucked up reasons. The world is a fucked up place, filled with fucked up people, who do fucked up things for fucked up reasons. The world is a fucked up place, filled with fucked up people, who do fucked up things for fucked up reasons. The world is a fucked up place, filled with fucked up people, who do fucked up things for fucked up reasons. The world is a fucked up place, filled with fucked up people, who do fucked up things for fucked up reasons. The world is a fucked up place, filled with fucked up people, who do fucked up things for fucked up reasons The world is a fucked up place, filled with fucked up people, who do fucked up things for fucked up reasons. The world is a fucked up place, filled with fucked up people, who do fucked up things for fucked up reasons. The world is a fucked up place, filled with fucked up people, who do fucked up things for fucked up reasons. The world is a fucked up place, filled with fucked up people, who do fucked up things for fucked up reasons.

The world is a fucked up place, filled with fucked up people, who do fucked up things for fucked up reasons. The world is a fucked up place, filled with fucked up people, who do fucked up things for fucked up reasons. The world is a fucked up place, filled with fucked up people, who do fucked up things for fucked up reasons. The world is a fucked up place, filled with fucked up people, who do fucked up things for fucked up reasons The world is a fucked up place, filled with fucked up people, who do fucked up things for fucked up reasons. The world is a fucked up place, filled with fucked up people, who do fucked up things for fucked up reasons. The world is a fucked up place, filled with fucked up people, who do fucked up things for fucked up reasons. The world is a fucked up place, filled with fucked up people, who do fucked up things for fucked up reasons. The world is a fucked up place, filled with fucked up people, who do fucked up things for fucked up reasons. The world is a fucked up place, filled with fucked up people, who do fucked up things for fucked up reasons. The world is a fucked up place, filled with fucked up people, who do fucked up things for fucked up reasons. The world is a fucked up place, filled with fucked up people, who do fucked up things for fucked up reasons The world is a fucked up place, filled with fucked up people, who do fucked up things for fucked up reasons. The world is a fucked up place, filled with fucked up people, who do fucked up things for fucked up reasons. The world is a fucked up place, filled with fucked up people, who do fucked up things for fucked up reasons. The world is a fucked up place, filled with fucked up people, who do fucked up things for fucked up reasons The world is a fucked up place, filled with fucked up people, who do fucked up things for fucked up reasons. The world is a fucked up place, filled with fucked up people, who do fucked up things for fucked up reasons. . The world is a fucked up place, filled with fucked up people, who do fucked up things for fucked up reasons. The world is a fucked up place, filled with fucked up people, who do fucked up things for fucked up reasons. The world is a fucked up place, filled with fucked up people, who do fucked up things for fucked up reasons. The world is a fucked up place, filled with fucked up people, who do fucked up things for fucked up reasons. The world is a fucked up place, filled with fucked up people, who do fucked up things for fucked up reasons. The world is a fucked up place, filled with fucked up people, who do fucked up things for fucked up reasons. The world is a fucked up place, filled with fucked up people, who do fucked up things for fucked up reasons. The world is a fucked up place, filled with fucked up people, who

do fucked up things for fucked up reasons. The world is a fucked up place, filled with fucked up people, who do fucked up things for fucked up reasons. The world is a fucked up place, filled with fucked up people, who do fucked up things for fucked up reasons. The world is a fucked up place, filled with fucked up people, who do fucked up things for fucked up reasons. The world is a fucked up place, filled with fucked up people, who do fucked up things for fucked up reasons. The world is a fucked up place, filled with fucked up people, who do fucked up things for fucked up reasons The world is a fucked up place, filled with fucked up people, who do fucked up things for fucked up reasons. The world is a fucked up place, filled with fucked up people, who do fucked up things for fucked up reasons. The world is a fucked up place, filled with fucked up people, who do fucked up things for fucked up reasons. The world is a fucked up place, filled with fucked up people, who do fucked up things for fucked up reasons. The world is a fucked up place, filled with fucked up people, who do fucked up things for fucked up reasons. The world is a fucked up place, filled with fucked up people, who do fucked up things for fucked up reasons. The world is a fucked up place, filled with fucked up people, who do fucked up things for fucked up reasons. The world is a fucked up place, filled with

fucked up people, who do fucked up things
for fucked up reasons The world is a fucked
up place, filled with fucked up people, who
do fucked up things for fucked up reasons.
The world is a fucked up place, filled with
fucked up people, who do fucked up things
for fucked up reasons. The world is a fucked
up place, filled with fucked up people, who
do fucked up things for fucked up reasons.
The world is a fucked up place, filled with
fucked up people, who do fucked up things
for fucked up reasons. The world is a fucked
up place, filled with fucked up people, who
do fucked up things for fucked up reasons.
The world is a fucked up place, filled with
fucked up people, who do fucked up things
for fucked up reasons The world is a fucked
up place, filled with fucked up people, who
do fucked up things for fucked up reasons.
The world is a fucked up place, filled with
fucked up people, who do fucked up things
for fucked up reasons. The world is a fucked
up place, filled with fucked up people, who
do fucked up things for fucked up reasons.
The world is a fucked up place, filled with
fucked up people, who do fucked up things
for fucked up reasons. The world is a fucked
up place, filled with fucked up people, who
do fucked up things for fucked up reasons.
The world is a fucked up place, filled with
fucked up people, who do fucked up things
for fucked up reasons. The world is a fucked

up place, filled with fucked up people, who do fucked up things for fucked up reasons. The world is a fucked up place, filled with fucked up people, who do fucked up things for fucked up reasons The world is a fucked up place, filled with fucked up people, who do fucked up things for fucked up reasons. The world is a fucked up place, filled with fucked up people, who do fucked up things for fucked up reasons. The world is a fucked up place, filled with fucked up people, who do fucked up things for fucked up reasons. The world is a fucked up place, filled with fucked up people, who do fucked up things for fucked up reasons. The world is a fucked up place, filled with fucked up people, who do fucked up things for fucked up reasons The world is a fucked up place, filled with fucked up people, who do fucked up things for fucked up reasons. The world is a fucked up place, filled with fucked up people, who do fucked up things for fucked up reasons. The world is a fucked up place, filled with fucked up people, who do fucked up things for fucked up reasons. The world is a fucked up place, filled with fucked up people, who do fucked up things for fucked up reasons. The world is a fucked up place, filled with fucked up people, who do fucked up things for fucked up reasons. The world is a fucked up place, filled with fucked up people, who do fucked up things for fucked up reasons.

The world is a fucked up place, filled with fucked up people, who do fucked up things for fucked up reasons. The world is a fucked up place, filled with fucked up people, who do fucked up things for fucked up reasons The world is a fucked up place, filled with fucked up people, who do fucked up things for fucked up reasons. The world is a fucked up place, filled with fucked up people, who do fucked up things for fucked up reasons. The world is a fucked up place, filled with fucked up people, who do fucked up things for fucked up reasons. The world is a fucked up place, filled with fucked up people, who do fucked up things for fucked up reasons. The world is a fucked up place, filled with fucked up people, who do fucked up things for fucked up reasons. The world is a fucked up place, filled with fucked up people, who do fucked up things for fucked up reasons.

I can keep going but really, if you don't have the words (if not their meaning) memorized by now you're obviously part of the problem

THE END

Postscript

If you disagree with my contentions and conclusions, a couple of quick questions...

Did you read the whole book or just a few pages then skipped ahead to THE END?

 Or, (and this is the more likely reason)

Do you feel you're just too advanced in your thinking to comprehend the obvious?

Either way   I'm going to give it one more try and this time let me spell it out for you

The world IS a F-U-C-K-E-D- U-P place, filled with F-U-C-K-E-D- U-P people, who do F-U-C-K-E-D- U-P things, for F-U-C-K-E-D- U-P reasons.

Acceptance of this fact doesn't make you a disengaged, disillusioned, cynic, nor does it answer the deeper question of why the world is such a fucked up place, filled with such fucked up people, who do such fucked up things for such fucked up reasons, but as Hilary Clinton once so famously said, "what difference does it (why) make!"

Some would say if you can't see the light you're living in the dark, but since perception is 9/10ths of reality; most people believe they are living in the shade.

You may be asking yourself how in this fucked up world, filled with fucked up people doing fucked up things for fucked up reasons do GOOD things happen? And though I haven't given that as much thought as I have to "why bad things happen" I think it's because people as fucked up as they are, are not inherently evil and good deeds fill the need in some to compensate for what their minds perceive as undeserved good fortune, but I'll have to think on it and get back to you. May be save that for another book

Well, that should do it, but should you feel the need feel free to continually carry this book, recite its core phrase again and again (a mantra of sorts) whenever your faith in humanity starts to resurface.

For now Please... Put this book down, (sign deeply) and just walk away.

www.ingramcontent.com/pod-product-compliance
Lightning Source LLC
Chambersburg PA
CBHW050505290526
45786CB00006B/2441